"All over this nation, God is stirring the hearts of men to rise up and enter into their God-given destiny. Lou Turner's lifelong passion is to see men enter into their divine purpose in life. 'Living Life God's Way,' of which this book is a part, is born out of this passion. Throughout this Bible study series, Turner opens up God's Word to help you discover HIS plan for your success in your life, family, and work. If you are ready to get off the treadmill, to begin to enjoy God's fullness in your life and make a significant contribution to the world around you, I recommend that you dive into this life-transforming Bible study."

Hal H. Sacks, D.Min., *BridgeBuilders International Leadership Network*

"It seems North American culture is rapidly moving toward what the Bible calls 'everyone doing what is right in his own mind' (Judges 21:25). The prophet Isaiah declared, 'Woe to those who call evil, good, and good, evil' (Isaiah 5:20). This Bible study series will challenge every man in the 21st century as 'iron sharpens iron'! The Q&As at the end of each chapter really personalize the teaching."

Dennis Conner, *Co-Founder/President, Called to Serve Prayer-Coaching Ministry*

"I have known Lou Turner for over twenty years. Lou loves Jesus and has built his life on the Word of God. Lou's Bible study series, 'Living Life God's Way,' is full of biblical truth that has been tested and can be applied by disciples of Jesus in practical ways. These books will help you grow in your faith and gain confidence and competence, which will increase your fruitfulness in Christ.

Mark Buckley, *Founding Pastor of Living Streams Church*

Living Life God's Way

Overcoming Strongholds

Lou Turner

Overcoming Strongholds
First Edition, 2020
Copyright © 2020 by Lou Turner

Overcoming Strongholds is part of the Living Life God's Way Series by Lou Turner.

All rights reserved. No part of this publication may be reproduced, stored in a retrieval system, or transmitted in any form by any means—electronic, mechanical, photocopy, recording, or otherwise—except for brief quotations in critical reviews or articles, without the prior permission of the publisher, except as provided by U.S. copyright law.

Unless otherwise identified, Scripture quotations are from the ESV® Bible (The Holy Bible, English Standard Version®), copyright © 2001 by Crossway, a publishing ministry of Good News Publishers. Used by permission. All rights reserved.

Scriptures marked NKJV are taken from the New King James Version, copyright 1982 by Thomas Nelson. Used by permission. All rights reserved.

Scripture quotations marked (NLT) are taken from the Holy Bible, New Living Translation, copyright ©1996, 2004, 2015 by Tyndale House Foundation. Used by permission of Tyndale House Publishers, Inc., Carol Stream, Illinois 60188. All rights reserved.

Some of the anecdotal illustrations in this book are true to life and are included with the permission of the persons involved. All other illustrations are composites of real situations, and any resemblance to people living or dead is coincidental.

To order additional books:
www.amazon.com
www.hislifeinus.com

ISBN: 978-1-7331186-4-4

Editorial and Book Packaging: Inspira Literary Solutions, Gig Harbor, WA
Book Design: PerfecType, Nashville, TN
Cover Design: MTWdesign, Dickson, TN
Printed in the USA by Ingram Spark

He will be like a tree firmly planted by streams of water,
Which yields its fruit in its season
And its leaf does not wither;
And in whatever he does, he prospers.

Psalm 1:3

TABLE OF CONTENTS

Preface ix

How to Use this Book xi

Introduction xiii

1. Strongholds and Spiritual Warfare 1

2. The Battle 15

3. Learning to Stand in Freedom 35

4. Weapons for the War 47

A Final Word 53

About the Author 55

PREFACE

We live in a world that has largely forgotten what manhood is about. In the Western world, men are often portrayed on television as buffoons who are out of touch and must rely on their wives to straighten them out. These characters are portrayed as silly, insensitive, lacking common sense, and when they do speak, they are generally wrong. They are generally portrayed as either ridiculously weak or overly macho. They are not able to commit to a long-term relationship and generally mistreat women. Positive role models are hard to find in the media.

However, the Bible teaches a different type of manhood, the authentic one. Men are to be leaders, loving their wives and children, excelling in their work, and standing for truth. They are to be men of wisdom, knowledge, having godly character and seeking after God and His direction. They are to be exhibiting godly leadership at church, in the community, and in business, and to be a light to those around them. They are to be men of compassion and love, as well as courageous and bold when needed.

Men go astray from these ideals, including Christian men, due to improper convictions or beliefs about life. They have received these from various sources: well-meaning family and friends, the media, and the culture around them—a world system that promotes the tearing down of God's biblical truths.

But without proper biblical foundation, we will all go astray.

PREFACE

That's why I wrote these books, containing insights, observations, and biblical truths distilled over the course of my decades of life and ministry. Each section is designed to be a stand-alone section for study and consideration. I hope this series, *Living Life God's Way*, will be used to disciple men in biblical truths for life. Whether you use it for yourself, with a group, or to mentor or disciple someone else, my hope is that it will be a blessing to you and encourage you to seek God and grow in Him.

HOW TO USE THIS BOOK

What does it mean to be a "good" husband and father?
How do I live out the Christian life at work?
What does God want from me—and how am I supposed to find that out?

These were questions that plagued me as a young man—questions, I learned, that are at the front of many men's minds at various times in their lives. For me, these questions began my quest to seek God and discover the answers, and my discoveries, over the years of my life, led to this series of booklets, *Living Life God's Way*. The series discusses 13 topics that every man must deal with, regardless of his work, calling, profession, or circumstances. It is difficult to know how to live the Christian life without understanding what God says about these areas of life.

These topics are:

1. Seeking and Finding God
2. Who You Are in Christ
3. A Man's Work and Ministry
4. Understanding Authority
5. A Man and His Wife
6. A Man and His Children
7. Getting Guidance From God

8. Overcoming Strongholds
9. A Man and Money
10. Repentance, Forgiveness, and Restitution
11. Being a Leader
12. Sex and Morality
13. The Test of Pride

You can use these books to study on your own, in a small group, or with a larger group of men. Each topic or booklet is a stand-alone study, and a person can begin with any one he chooses. They are different lengths and can be adapted to various settings—home, church, or community—all topics that are pertinent to today.

Explore what the Bible says about these important and critical areas. The encouragement is to read these with an open heart, asking God to reveal His truth to you in each of these areas of life. Pray that His Spirit will show you His truth, so that you may live in it and enjoy all God has for you. I pray that you experience the blessing and presence of God in your life as you draw closer to Him and more aware of His leading in every area of your life.

INTRODUCTION TO OVERCOMING STRONGHOLDS

Anyone who has been a follower of Jesus for any length of time has surely realized that our capacity for sin does not evaporate when we receive Christ. As long as we are in these earthy bodies, we will struggle with sin. Even the Apostle Paul struggled with this, and wrote:

> *". . . I do not understand my own actions. For I do not do what I want, but I do the very thing I hate. . . . So now it is no longer I who do it, but sin that dwells within me. For I know that nothing good dwells in me, that is, in my flesh. For I have the desire to do what is right, but not the ability to carry it out. . . . For I delight in the law of God, in my inner being, but I see in my members another law waging war against the law of my mind and making me captive to the law of sin that dwells in my members. Wretched man that I am! Who will deliver me from this body of death?? (Romans 7:15-24, condensed)*

If the Scriptures left us here, we would not have much hope. But Paul goes on to say in Romans 8:1-2, *"Therefore there is now no condemnation for those who are in Christ Jesus, because through*

INTRODUCTION TO OVERCOMING STRONGHOLDS

Christ Jesus the law of the Spirit of life set me free from the law of sin and death." In this, we see that God recognizes we are tempted and that we may struggle with temptation. But He clearly states that He has provided His Spirit to live in us to give us the ability to be set free from the power of sin in our lives.

Temptation and spiritual attacks are a part of every Christian's life. However, "strongholds" are more than this; they are areas where we are continually living in compromise, where we are not living according to God's Word and are settling for less than God has for us. In this case, there is a pattern and a history in our life of giving into these areas and living our life in compromise. Strongholds seem to have a hold on us beyond the normal temptations and struggles with the flesh spoken about in Romans 7; we have likely been living this way for some time and the pattern is ingrained in our lives. Because of this, our thinking, our hearts, and our habits are deeply affected. Becoming convinced that God wants us to be free of bondage is critical. We must agree with Scripture in our hearts. We need to become convinced that God wants us to be free; that's what His Word, the Bible, tells us. When we understand this, we can take the steps to become free, realizing that God is prepared to help us and give us the ability both to *get* free and *stay* free. God wants us to walk in His freedom, and not be bound to anything that keeps us from His best for us.

The enemy is well aware of our weaknesses. He tempts us and does all he can to keep us in bondage. Nevertheless, we have been called and equipped to live in victory over sin, and to defeat any strongholds in our lives.

Chapter 1

STRONGHOLDS AND SPIRITUAL WARFARE

We all find ourselves battling against temptation, don't we? We struggle with being too critical, being angry when we shouldn't, getting discouraged, or having our hopes dashed. But for many, if not most of us, there are those seemingly lifelong battles, places we never seem to be able to conquer or gain victory. These may be our "secret sins," the ones we don't want to talk about.

For example, many men have a continual battle with lust and their thought lives—not just normal temptation, but a constant struggle. Others may have a critical spirit; they continually criticize others and find fault with almost everyone. Still others may live in ongoing fear of some event happening to them now or in the future. These are common struggles and we may all struggle with these at times. But with some, we may find ourselves in a never-ending battle, cycling up and down emotionally as we try to gain victory and then feel defeated yet again.

When we consider these problem areas, the questions that demand answers are, "Can the struggle with fear, depression, pornography, addictions, or _____ (you fill in the blank) be broken? Can Christians live in victory where they have been living in defeat—sometimes for years?" The answer to both questions is ***yes***.

At 2:00 a.m. one morning, I was awakened by the Lord and felt impressed to get out of bed and pray. As I prayed, thoughts came into my mind of areas I had struggled with for years and in which I had no lasting victory. Then I began to consider scriptures that said I was to walk in victory, not constantly struggling over the same problems. The stage was set.

On the one hand, I was painfully aware of the pattern of repeated defeat; on the other hand, I was aware of scriptures that said I was to walk in victory. I had prayed and claimed this victory for myself—and sometimes even had short-lived success—but then I fell back into old up and down patterns.

I had lived most of my adult life with these ups-and-downs; a pattern of partial victory and defeat, and I was tired of it. That night I cried out, "God, where is Your delivering power? Why can't I experience victory and freedom? Is Your Word real or not? If it is real, why isn't it real in my life?"

Many, if not most, Christians secretly battle such problem areas. A biblical term we can use for these persistent problems that seem to dominate our lives is a *stronghold*. We see in 2 Corinthians 10:3-5 that a stronghold is a pattern of wrong thinking, raised up against the truth of God, and that God has given us "divinely powerful weapons" to fight against them. As I cried out to God that night, He began to reveal to me that the issues troubling me were strongholds from which He wanted me to be free. It was time to stand, pray about them, and persist until I gained lasting victory.

Fortified and Defended

In the Old Testament, strongholds were fortified places intended to defend against the enemy. David stayed in strongholds when he was fleeing from King Saul so he would be better able to defend himself.

In the New Testament, the word *strongholds* is used in 2 Corinthians 10:4, *"For the weapons of our warfare are not of the flesh, but have divine power to destroy strongholds."* Since the "strongholds" referred to here need to be pulled down with spiritual weapons, this clearly refers to strongholds we need to be free of—strongholds of the flesh and of the enemy, Satan, and his forces.

Satan tries to establish strongholds and to defend his turf—places where he has gained a foothold. Satan continually works to fortify strongholds in locations, in cultures, in governments, and in individuals—including Christians. Strongholds can exist over villages, cities, or nations where some type of sin has a great influence or stranglehold. For the purposes of this study, we will focus on strongholds in the lives of individuals.

This is not talking about Christians being possessed by demons; rather, it means believers feel like they are controlled or plagued in certain areas of their lives by negative thoughts, behaviors, and attitudes. Satan and his forces are aware of these vulnerable areas and try to capitalize on them to keep the Christian weak and bound. Satan is the accuser. He accuses us and wants us to feel defeated and unworthy. This is the battle he wages against us, i.e., spiritual warfare.

How Strongholds Form

Strongholds are areas where sinful actions, attitudes, or desires have established a hold in our lives. They are usually founded on a pattern of thinking or actions that have taken root in our heart. These practices have become ingrained in us for a variety of reasons; they have become part not only of our behavior, but often our worldview. Even though we sometimes struggle against them, trying to overcome strongholds in our own strength or willpower, they remain like the walls of a fort and we seem unable to bring them down.

Strongholds can also be a carry over from our life prior to salvation when we lived our life contrary to God's Word. At some point in our lives, we gave in to sin and a pattern developed of yielding to it over and over again. So, these behaviors or thought patterns became a part of us. We may be aware of our struggle or it can be a blind spot, something others can see but we are blind to. If it is a blind spot, it may be so ingrained that it may take God, either sovereignly or speaking through another person, to reveal it to us.

But not all strongholds come as a result of our choices or being a willing participant in certain activities. Strongholds of the mind, or false philosophy—believing things that are unscriptural—can come from our culture, our upbringing, or from false teaching.

Other strongholds can come from abuse or molestation. Many people have deep hurts, fears, bitterness, or even hatred due to hurtful things that were done to them. Children who have been molested have deep wounds that need to be healed. Wives who have been battered or mistreated carry deep wounds. And both men and women whose spouses have been unfaithful may carry deep hurt from feeling betrayed or rejected.

People who have been swindled or cheated in business or who have been verbally abused by someone they love, or someone in authority over them, suffer the effects of those wounds and often have great hesitancy to move forward or to trust again. Many people have been let down or disappointed by those they admired—including their pastors or other spiritual leaders.

These things keep us from living the victorious life of being motivated by love and trust in God. They kill our joy. They rob of us our peace. They can cause doubt, a feeling of wanting to give up, or a passive acceptance of current circumstances as "our life," with no real hope of change.

Often, a stronghold contains a mix of causes. We may have been hurt or wounded, and then give in to a temptation to seek comfort in an addiction, or to become bitter or vengeful. If you don't care to call it a stronghold, then you can simply call it an area where you are not living in God's freedom for you. Some of these are easily overcome; others can take time and seeking God for freedom and healing.

For example, Shaun was a Christian who loved the Lord and desired to please Him in his life. However, he had a real problem with a critical spirit. He found fault in most people and was critical of almost everyone. He had few friends because no one "measured up." When he met with his boss one day, his boss stated he was a hard worker who had excellent results in his job, but was constantly finding fault with his fellow workers. He told him to be more tolerant and to remember that no one was perfect.

Because he was a Christian, this conversation should have convicted Shaun and caused him to seek God to change his heart. However, he rejected his boss' counsel and the problem remained. He continued to have few friends, and he pulled away from church attendance.

Later, in counseling, he confessed he had a very difficult time accepting himself and believing God loved him. Being critical of himself and feeling unloved caused him to have a critical spirit toward others. As he saw others' faults, he felt better about himself and his imperfections. He was truly bound in this pattern of tearing down himself and others.

Until he realized he had a critical spirit, he could not be set free from it. He had to see it as sin, repent of it, and look to God to reveal His love and forgiveness for him and to heal him. Shaun also needed to break the pattern of being critical of others. Yet, until he wanted to be free, he would not seek God to free him.

Strongholds can become such a part of our lives that we are reluctant to deal with them. While God wants us to be free and has provided the weapons by which we gain that freedom, the first step to freedom begins with us. We have to recognize the problem and want to be free from it.

Freedom Begins with Us

God's love, His grace, and the power of His Spirit are present to help us, heal us, and lead us to victory in overcoming strongholds, or areas of constant struggle. Our part is to look to God for His provision of being set free. We can be free! We can walk in freedom!

Matthew 19 tells the story of the rich young ruler who came to Christ asking what he must do to advance spiritually. Jesus looked into his heart and dealt with the issue that was holding him back—materialism and the love of money. He told the rich young ruler, *"If you want to be perfect [complete], go, sell what you have and give to the poor, and you will have treasure in heaven; and come, follow Me"* (Matthew 19:21).

The young man came to Christ but was unwilling to follow this directive, and so his area of bondage remained. It wasn't that having wealth was wrong. It was the place money and wealth had in his heart.

God's Word is clear that we, who are in Christ, are already free from sin and "complete." **When we accepted Christ as our Savior, we obtained all He has for us.** Colossians 2:9-10 says, *"For in Him dwells all the fullness of the Godhead bodily; and you are complete in Him, who is the head of all principality and power."* Christ is the head of *all* principalities and power and we are already "complete" in Him.

The Apostle Paul's goal and prayer was to present every man "perfect" or "complete" in Christ Jesus. *"Him we preach, warning every man and teaching every man in all wisdom, that we may present every man perfect in Christ Jesus"* (Colossians 1:28). The word *perfect* here means "complete or whole."

We are complete positionally (that is, in our position with God through Christ) at salvation. We have inherited all Christ has for us at that point. But we must also obtain it practically. Our inheritance needs to be a part of our daily life. This happens as we come to realize, to know, what God wants for our life. We become complete, obtaining all Christ has for us, as we know His will for us and begin to claim it and live it for our life.

Claiming it is two-fold. One, we seek God and ask Him to make it real in our life. We recognize our need and seek Him to change us. Two, we choose to believe it is ours and begin to think differently and act differently. Meditating on scriptures that deal with the area we are believing God to change is powerful. We begin to meditate, think on, the truth and it begins to be a part of us. Since we know the Bible is God's Word and what it says is truth for us, we can rely on its truth and claim it for our life.

Paul expounded on this theme when he wrote to believers at Philippi: *"Being confident of this very thing, that **he** who has begun a good work in you will complete it until the day of Jesus Christ"* (Philippians 1:6, emphasis added). Until Christ comes back, it is God's purpose to work in us to finish the work He has started.

However, even though we have inherited all Christ has for us, we may not be living in that victory or provision. It's like we have received a great inheritance, but do not know how to access it or use it. It is not a matter of whether He has power to free us, it is a matter of us coming into agreement with Him and wanting to walk according to His will.

We have to understand what is ours, and we have to want it, desire it, more than the things that are holding us back. Then we must be willing to fight the good fight of faith and obtain that which is ours. Consider the following verses:

> *For this reason we also, since the day we heard it, do not cease to pray for you, and to ask that you may be filled with the knowledge of His will in all wisdom and spiritual understanding; that you may have a walk worthy of the Lord, fully pleasing Him, being fruitful in every good work and increasing in the knowledge of God; strengthened with all might, according to His glorious power, for all patience and longsuffering with joy; giving thanks to the Father who has qualified us to be partakers of the inheritance of the saints in the light.* ***He has delivered us from the power of the darkness and translated us into the kingdom of the Son of His love, in whom we have redemption, through His blood, the forgiveness of sins.*** *(Colossians 1:9-14, emphasis added)*

Jesus, through His finished work on the cross, has delivered us from the power of darkness and translated us into the kingdom of God. We should not settle for less.

I knew two men, Ted and his boss Gary, who were traveling by car on a business trip. Gary recognized Ted as hard working and conscientious and believed he had a good future with the company. Since it would take a few hours to reach their destination, they were talking about a mixture of business and spiritual matters. Both Ted and Gary were Christians and active in their churches. Ted, a former pastor, had been in ministry most of his life. However, he had lost his family and his ministry. His wife had left him for another man and taken his children; after that, he was removed from his ministry position. These events had hurt him deeply.

Ted was now ministering on a volunteer basis in the singles ministry of a sizeable church, and the conversation turned to his ministry activities. That's when Ted began to confess that he had been sexually involved with some of the women in his singles group. Gary, who was also in a leadership position in a church, was somewhat taken aback and began to encourage Ted to break off any unhealthy relationships. Ted became defensive and said, "It's easy for you to say that. You're married and have a wife. I don't and I'm lonely. What about my needs?"

Gary said he understood Ted's desire for companionship, but Ted was approaching it wrong. He reminded him what God's Word said about immoral relationships, and that he was in a leadership role in a large church, and much was at stake. Ted, however, defended his actions and finally changed the subject.

Gary was burdened for Ted. The next time they were together, Gary asked how he was doing in relationships, and Ted continued to be defensive. Whenever the subject came up over the next few months, he seemed unrepentant. He was settling for less than God desired for him. He eventually lost his position in the church as his actions came to light. At this time, he was not willing to fight that "good fight of faith."

Strongholds Cannot Prevail

Victory over difficult areas can be won, but we must be willing to battle, to enter into spiritual warfare. God is going to do the work as we determine to persist until we gain victory. We begin the battle through prayer and Bible study to convince us that victory is God's will for us. Once we realize that freedom is God's will and purpose, we can pray with greater confidence, asking God to accomplish His will and bring us that freedom. As we do our part, God will certainly do His. God will change the very desires of our heart so we will not desire the areas of sin that have plagued us if we are sincere and seek Him to do just that.

We have to actively participate in gaining our freedom. A major source of gaining victory is to begin to confess who you are in Christ. The Bible tells us many things about ourselves. It says we are the righteousness of Christ, we are forgiven and loved, we are redeemed and set free from sin, and we are the beloved of Christ. These are just some of the things said about us regarding our position in Christ. As we confess these things, these truths come alive in us and begin to transform us. Because it is Bible truth, it impacts us positively.

If you go about confessing these things, it is difficult for sin and past strongholds to dominate you. In fact, you will be able to dominate them and have victory over them. You will be confessing the truth of God's word and it will stir in you the life of Christ through the Holy Spirit who lives in you.

In Matthew 16:18, Jesus was talking about the truth that had just been revealed to Peter—that Jesus was the Messiah. Jesus said, *"On this rock* [the truth of who Jesus was and the work He has done for us] *I will build My church, and the gates of Hades shall not prevail against it."*

Gates can be used to keep the enemy out or to keep someone bound in prison. The gates of Hades were to keep captives from escaping—to keep them bound. Jesus was saying that the gates of Hades or Hell would not be able to hold out against the truth of the gospel and keep people imprisoned. Because of Christ's redeeming work on the cross, the Church, as it walked in the truth, would be able to spoil the kingdom of Satan and tear down the gates or defenses of his strongholds.

God continued to work in Ted's heart. Sometime later, Ted and Gary were together again, and this time Ted brought up the subject. He said, "I realize I can't be free in this area until I want to be. I am asking God to change my heart, and I am going to Him for freedom."

Ted, whom I mentioned earlier, did pick up his battle again. He determined to follow after God daily with a renewed focus and to cut off the physical relationships he had been entertaining. He asked the women he had been involved with for forgiveness. During the next year, God brought great healing in Ted's life. At the end of the year, he met a Christian woman, fell in love, and they were married. Their marriage was successful and Christ-centered. As he followed God, he obtained what he wanted from the Lord—a godly and loving wife.

God wants us to be delivered from the kingdom of darkness into the kingdom of light—His kingdom. God's kingdom here on Earth consists of living His way, doing things His way, and having a relationship with God Himself. It is thinking and being who God wants us to be. Satan wants us to settle for less and live a life of compromise. God wants our minds—our thinking—to be renewed, and our hearts changed. He wants us to realize what He thinks of us and what He wants for us. This is God's will and purpose for us.

The Bible states that we will be transformed by renewing our minds. It says, *"Do not be conformed to this world, but be transformed by the renewing of your mind, that you may prove what is that good and acceptable will of God"* (Romans 12:2). This is a powerful statement. A changed mind transforms our heart, and when our mind and heart are changed, we change. As we meditate on God's truth about our life and pray for God to make it real in us, the Spirit will do just that. We will be transformed and renewed, and the stronghold that binds us will be broken. As we pray over this—repeatedly if needed—we will see God's power released in us. The stronghold's power over us will be less and less, and the victory of God's Spirit will be more and more.

Seeking God, having our mind be renewed, and experiencing change in our heart are really important steps. What we are saying is that we realize we do not trust our hearts to always want what is right. It is also an admission that we need to have our minds renewed and our hearts changed so we will change.

When we ask God to renew our mind and change our heart, we are asking Him to help us turn away—that is, help us "not to choose"—the things that are wrong for our life. As we turn our mind and heart over to God, He works in us, changing our very desires.

When we ask God to renew our mind and change our heart, we will no longer want the things that are wrong for our life. As we renew our mind and turn our heart over to God, He will cause our heart to come into alignment with His desires for us and it will break the power of any sin in our life. The work Jesus did will take hold in our life and become real in us.

If we truly want to be free, we can be free as we surrender to God and seek after Him and His truth.

QUESTIONS FOR REFLECTION AND DISCUSSION

1. Are there areas of struggle in your life where you can't seem to get free? What are they?

   _____

   _____

   _____

2. Which of the following have you thought regarding these areas? Mark all that apply.
   ____ I will never get free.
   ____ This is just the way I am; I have no option.
   ____ I deserve to indulge in _____ because life is difficult in other ways.
   ____ Everyone seems to live with these areas; this is mine, and I just have to deal with it.
   ____ I can't let anyone know about this—especially other Christians. I must keep this hidden.
   ____ I've done everything I can do about this, and just given up.
   ____ Other _____

3. Do you truly want to be free? Do you think you have been holding on to anything that can be hindering you from being set free? If so, what is it?

   _____

   _____

   _____

   _____

4. Do you believe in your heart that God wants to set you free, that He wants you to walk in freedom and victory? If so, write below your declaration of God's desire to free you and write out what He wants you to be free of.

_____

_____

_____

_____

TAKE A KNEE

Let's kneel before the Lord and pray. If you are physically unable to kneel, then kneel to God in your heart:

"Dear Father, I want to be free in any area of my life where I am living in a manner that is less than Your will. I ask You to reveal to me anything that is hindering my freedom. Reveal to me the truth of Your Word regarding my freedom. Let it take root in my heart. Convince me that this truth is for me and that You are ready and willing to work in my life to bring me freedom.

Your Word and Your truth is for me, personally, and not just for others. I confess that Jesus has won the victory for me, and that He desires me to be free. I purpose to seek You for all You have for me. I don't want to settle for less. Thank You, Father, for Your love, Your forgiveness, Your grace, and Your sacrifice for me."

Chapter 2

The Battle

Jack was a believer with a heart for God. One day he was sitting in his office when he sensed God calling him to prayer. He asked his secretary to hold his calls, closed his door, and began to pray.

He had been wondering why he was struggling in certain areas and had been praying about it. As he sat in his office and prayed, he sensed God's presence, and God's Spirit began to show him how his heart was divided.

God brought to mind immoral relationships that he'd had as a young man before he gave his life to God. The Lord showed him that he harbored pleasant memories of many of these times and looked upon them, in his heart, as times of pleasure and fun. God convicted him that he needed to recognize and acknowledge that these immoral relationships were sin and harmful to his life, and that they had opened the door to a pattern of immorality in his past life. This pattern had established a stronghold that now, years later, was still affecting him.

Jack was a married man by now and loved his wife. He was not involved in immoral relationships with other women, but he was involved with struggles in his heart regarding lust. Because he still looked upon these past relationships with fondness, a foothold had been established in his heart of accepting the immoral relationships of his past.

If you asked him, he would say they were wrong. But in his heart, he was not able to come to grips that these relationships were harmful to his life. After all, if these relationships had brought pleasure and caused him to feel desired by women, then they had brought a measure of satisfaction to his need for love and acceptance. However, he had looked for love and acceptance in the wrong places and had compromised God's standard for his life. This had established a pattern and stronghold in his heart and thinking.

All men face temptation morally. Jesus did also, but did not yield to it and so did not sin. Temptation is not sin. Giving into it is. If we have established a pattern of giving into temptation in any area, it must be broken and a new pattern established.

It is important to realize that temptation is not sin. Neither is it participating in sin for impure thoughts to enter your mind. It is what we do with the temptation and the thoughts that is important. We can reject them or entertain them. As soon as we realize we are thinking on things that we should not be, we can reject them and begin to think on good things. As one man said, "You can't keep a bird from flying over your head. But you can prevent it from making a nest there."

The Bible tells us to render our thoughts to God. This means to reject bad or sinful thoughts and choose to think on good things. We cannot dwell on harmful and sinful things without it affecting us. When we have sinful or harmful thoughts enter our mind, we can begin to pray and render these harmful thoughts to God and reject them.

> *"Since you have been raised with Christ, set your hearts on things above, where Christ is, seated at the right hand of God. Set your minds on the things above, not on earthly things . . . Put to death therefore, whatever belongs to your earthly nature: sexual immorality, impurity, lust, evil desires and greed"* (Colossians 3:1-3, 5)
>
> *"Whatever is true, whatever is noble, whatever is right, whatever is pure, whatever is lovely, whatever is admirable- if anything is excellent or praiseworthy-think about such things"* (Philippians 4:8).

The apostle Paul realized the need to do this. So what he is saying in the passages is this: Don't think on things that are bad for your life or sinful. You have the power and ability to stop thinking about negative things and decide to think on good things. If this were not possible, the Bible would not instruct us to do so.

I remember standing on a street in Dallas, Texas one day when an attractive woman walked by. Thoughts began to enter my mind and I felt utterly defeated. I thought, "I will never be free of impure thoughts." I have come to realize that in this life, I will be subject to temptation and will have impure thoughts enter my mind. I have also come to realize I don't have to entertain them—I can reject them—and my fellowship with God is not broken because of temptation. Do I stumble at times? Yes. But when I realize I have done so, I confess it, accept my forgiveness, and accept that my fellowship with God is intact.

While all Christians face temptation and are aware of shortcomings in their lives, an area where we are living in defeat, or a stronghold, is evidence that we are being controlled to some extent. In some cases, the stronghold may influence us greatly. If we are bound or controlled in an area, it not only affects us, but can also affect our families or others around us.

The Lord showed Jack that until he recognized these past relationships for what they were and asked forgiveness for them, he could never have a whole heart to give to the Lord and to his wife. He had given pieces of his heart along the way to other women. God could not heal Jack's heart and make it whole again until he gave up these memories and recognized them for what they were—immoral relationships that were not God's will. Jack was harboring secret and improper feelings.

Jack repented there in his office and asked God to forgive him not only for the acts, but also for the way he had viewed them. He asked God to heal his heart and restore it, make it whole, so he could give it fully first to God and then to his wife. This began a healing process in the areas in which he had been struggling.

The Process

Jack's story illustrates how God often begins the process of freeing us from long-standing strongholds. As we become more and more aware of a stronghold, most of us will begin to try to change and overcome the problem by willpower or by personal resolve.

That's when the roller coaster begins—days of getting better and days of defeat. In time, despair or great discouragement may set in and we may feel that there is no answer for us. But there is, and it lies in following God's plan for victory, and not relying on our own human effort. Let's look at steps we can take toward freedom:

1. Take a Stand for Freedom

First, take several steps with God in prayer:

- Identify the area of struggle and confess it to God.
- Ask God to reveal if any underlying problems are hindering you from obtaining your freedom (like Jack did).
- If appropriate, ask God's forgiveness for harboring inappropriate thoughts or feelings in your heart. This could be things such as harboring unforgiveness, being bitter, pursuing wrong or immoral relationships, being critical, or slandering others.
- Confess God's love for you, His forgiveness, and His grace given to you. Ask God for His healing. Begin to thank Him for the victory He is granting. Speak the truth of God's Word that you are God's child, that Christ died to set you free, and that you don't have to live this way. Begin to confess who you are in Christ. Speak it aloud. Declare it is for you.
- Start to think differently. This is really, really important. When thoughts come to our mind that are unscriptural or wrong, we must stop thinking about them, or change the way we think about them according to God's Word.

If a lustful thought comes, we can purpose to stop thinking about it, and we can begin to pray and thank God for delivering us. We can begin to establish new thought patterns and thus, break off the old ones. We can completely change our thought patterns and our hearts attitudes by practicing this and asking God to help us. We will talk more about this.

2. Stand Firm in Your Freedom

After you have taken the above steps:

- Ask God to show you how to stand in freedom in this area.
- Pray over this daily, confess that God's Word is true, and ask God to change your heart, renew your mind, and heal you. Declare this several times a day. It will happen as you seek God for it.
- Look up scriptures that deal with this life issue. Meditate on them and memorize one or more. Graft the truth of these scriptures into your heart and mind so you become convinced of their truth. You will be surprised at what will happen when you memorize Scripture and meditate on it. It will bring change and healing into your life.

You have a choice to make: begin to take steps to be free or continue to live the old way, the way that is less than God's best for you. If you truly want to be free, then go for it by going for God and His will for you. Changing our perspective by agreeing with God's Word and beginning to change our thinking will change us.

Sin, Forgiveness, and Grace

As Jack's story illustrates, **there can be pleasure in sin. But all sin, even sin that seems pleasurable at the moment, brings a price with it.** Sin must be taken to God so we can receive His forgiveness. When I speak of asking for forgiveness for sin, I am not talking about getting saved again, but rather confessing before God that we are engaged in actions, attitudes, or behaviors that the Bible states are wrong. We are admitting that our behavior or attitudes are wrong and we are coming into agreement with God.

It is true that because of the work Jesus did at the cross, we were forgiven for all of our past, present, and future sins. We received this forgiveness when we accepted Christ as our Savior.

In Him, we are forgiven and clean. So why confess it and ask forgiveness? We need to call it what it is: sin.

We need to confess that it is not God's will for us to live in it. We need to confess that Jesus paid the price for us to be free and that His work provided what we need to overcome sin. We need to confess that we are going to seek God for His victory in our life and keep on seeking Him daily till we receive it.

We need to ask forgiveness for choosing to live in this area or stronghold, and letting it have such a strong influence in our life. And, we need to realize that any area of sin that we continually participate in affects us and our relationship with God and others. We need to ask God to change our hearts so that this area no longer has a hold on us. If necessary, we need to pray this several times a day until it becomes real in our life.

When we became Christians, the work Jesus did for us on the cross provided forgiveness for all our sin—past, present, and future. Christ's blood washed us clean; we are no longer "sinners," we are now the "righteousness of Christ" (2 Corinthians 5:21), although sometimes that is hard to grasp. We are washed clean of our sin and, through Christ's work, are to have victory over it.

However, if we continue to participate or practice in things that are wrong, it will hinder our lives and afflict our hearts and souls. And, because it affects our hearts and souls, it can in turn affect our relationship with God. God stands ready to forgive and restore us, but if we continue to pursue things we should not, it will affect us, possibly greatly, depending on what it is. That's why, if a stronghold has bound us and we are in a battle with an attitude or behavior the Bible states is wrong, we need to be freed from that pattern. Jesus died for us to be free.

> *What shall we say then? Shall we continue in sin that grace may abound? Certainly not! How shall we who died to sin live any longer in it? Or do you not know that as many of*

> us as were baptized into Christ Jesus were baptized into His death? Therefore we were buried with Him through baptism into death, that just as Christ was raised from the dead by the glory of the Father, even so we also should walk in newness of life. (Romans 6:1-4)

We are not sentenced to be in bondage to any sin. This scripture clearly says that we have been granted freedom from bondage to sin—freedom from strongholds. Colossians 1:13 says that God *"has delivered us from the power of darkness and translated us into the kingdom of the Son of His love, in whom we have redemption, through His blood, the forgiveness of sins."*

Christ's grace toward us (His unmerited favor) is present to work in us. Often, just understanding God's love and grace toward us can break strongholds and bring great freedom. When we do not understand God's love and acceptance, we think we have to earn His love or work to get Him to bestow His grace on us. Nothing can be farther from the truth.* God's love and forgiveness are for all of our past, present, and future sins. When the light of this truth breaks upon us, the stronghold begins to be destroyed. We come to realize that God wants us to be free.

Spiritual Warfare

As we begin to battle a stronghold, we can expect to encounter a spiritual battle. Part of the spiritual warfare is getting our hearts and thinking changed so that we agree with God.

As we begin to war against a specific area by praying over it daily, we will see God work. This is spiritual warfare: seeking

---

*Another study in this series, *Who You Are in Christ*, discusses in detail who we are and who we are becoming in Christ, and all He has done to set us free.

God's will for us, agreeing with it, and praying for it to be done while we resist the enemy as he tries to discourage us, seduce, or defeat us. Then we obey what God reveals to us as His will.

As we pray for His will to be done—in this case, for us to be free—He may show us things we must do or certain ways to pray. We may have to ask for forgiveness and forgive others, ask Him to change our hearts, and eliminate activities that bring temptation.

Be aware, Satan does not want to give up this ground. He will continue to tempt us in the area we are striving for freedom. But as we practice right behavior and right thinking, we will begin to walk in victory and the "pull" of the old area of struggle will lessen more and more. God's Spirit is always with us to help us.

Timing and Process

At times, God will instantly set people free from bondage to strongholds—including addictions. But that is not always the pattern. Since our hearts and minds (or thought patterns) are involved, we often get victory as we realize the truth, claim it, and pursue it. In 1 Timothy 2:4 we see that God our Savior *"desires all people to be saved and to come to the knowledge of the truth."* As we align ourselves with Him by agreeing with the truth, and surrender for Him to do His work in us, we become free. Our victory will grow as we continue to allow God to change us and as we practice new thinking and pursue new behaviors.

Some things happen as soon as we begin to agree with God and confess the truth. The stronghold may just "fall away," so to speak. At other times, as we enter into the spiritual warfare of standing against the enemy and claiming the truth, we begin a longer process toward victory. The freedom will come.

Some people may need counseling in order to break free from deeply entrenched addictions and harmful habits. However, counselors need to counsel according to God's Word. Many counselors, although sincere, can hinder the process or confuse the truth. Counsel that does not agree with biblical truths and principles is not good counsel.

Tangled Roots

Sometimes, stronghold are connected to other areas that must be dealt with before freedom can come. Bitterness, anger, and hatred may be tied to unforgiveness and deep hurt. Lust can be tied to past immorality that we are harboring in our hearts. Fear can be tied to abuse or other past experiences for which we need to receive healing in our hearts and emotions.

Many people have trouble trusting God because of past hurts and disappointments, especially if it came from a Christian leader they looked up to. Others have allowed themselves to harbor hurt or bitterness over the loss of a loved one, a divorce, abuse, or a traumatic circumstance. **If you have been abused, it was not God's will for you. People do things that are not God's will. God wants to heal you of these hurts and bondages and wants you to be free.**

The fact that people let us down does not mean that God will; He is faithful. We must be willing to lay these hurts before Him, choose to trust Him, and allow Him to reveal His love for us and bring healing to us.

We may have to allow God to show us the roots of certain habits, attitudes, or desires that need to be confessed and forsaken before He can free us. Many times these roots are the reason we do not get immediate deliverance from our stronghold. God may have a deeper work to do in us. We need to allow Him to do this work by revealing the roots of the problem. This will give us greater understanding, insight, and eventually a greater ability to help others.

I am not talking about constant introspection and looking at our faults. That will only depress us. God does not burden us by making us beg Him for His victory and help. His burden is light and His yoke easy (Matthew 11:30).

While at times we may need to understand how things that happened in the past have affected us so we can put it behind us and claim freedom, constantly delving into your past and blaming others for your problems and shortcomings is unhealthy. We have to accept what has happened and get beyond it. If we need to forgive for things of the past, then we should forgive and not dwell on it. Dwelling on the past is not only unhealthy, it can be dangerous to our spiritual health.

We should ask God to grant us the insights we need so we will understand how any areas of struggle has come about in our life. He wants to enlighten us and free us. He does not send us down some complicated maze where we stumble about, get discouraged, and give up. He will lead us to freedom when we take on "His yoke," which is to walk in step with Him.

Focusing on the past and constantly reliving the past is harmful. We need to focus on God's love, forgiveness and the healing He desires for our life.

Laying our lives before Him and asking Him to heal us, and then beginning to pray for victory is the start to freedom. Reading and even memorizing Scripture regarding the particular area of struggle will hasten our healing as we learn God's truth.

Walking the Walk

Beginning to practice walking in the truth brings on a new life for us. The Lord does not want us to continue to walk in darkness, but in the light. In my own life, I have become free of things that were a part of my life for years as I simply determined to change the way I thought about things. Let me give you an example.

I used to have a real problem with a critical attitude toward others. I would find fault and criticize others for what I thought were their "shortcomings." One day, the Lord showed me this critical attitude was wrong. It put barriers between others and me and kept me from having many good relationships with others. When the Lord showed me this (it was a real blind spot in my life; I thought it was normal), I asked Him to forgive me for harboring this attitude toward others and I purposed to change. Then as critical attitudes and thoughts came into my mind, I purposed not to think these thoughts, and many times began to pray for those people.

As I began to practice not entertaining these critical thoughts and instead determining to be a person of encouragement to others, my attitudes and heart began to change. The stronghold was broken. Does that mean I never have critical thoughts I should not have? No. But now they are easier recognize and to dismiss. I feel a greater compassion for others and a greater desire to encourage others. The former stronghold has given way to a greater desire to reach out to others. The weakness of being critical of others has turned into a greater love for them. I have become a greater "grace giver" and less a condemner.

In the same way, as we begin to practice thinking differently and acting differently, strongholds will fall away and in their place new grace gifts will begin to bear fruit in us. God's grace and the indwelling power of His Spirit will begin to strengthen and empower us as we begin to practice attitudes and actions that agree with scripture and God's will for us. His Word and His Spirit break the strongholds as we simply begin to practice truth. We turn away from wrong and practice right. *"For just as you presented your members as slaves to impurity and to lawlessness, resulting in further lawlessness, so now present your members as slaves to righteousness, resulting in sanctification"* (Romans 6:19).

As we practice new thinking and new actions, we are presenting ourselves (our members) to righteousness. The result is sanctification, or a change in us. We will not be the same, we will change. We will walk in freedom where we were walking in bondage. We will rejoice in God's goodness and faithfulness!

God's Truth

The Bible is not just words. God's Word is *"living and powerful, and sharper than any two edged sword, piercing even to the division of soul and spirit, and of joints and marrow, and is a discerner of the thoughts and intents of the heart"* (Hebrews 4:12).

As we read and consider Scripture, God's Spirit will reveal our mindsets and the condition, or "intents," of our hearts. He will give us discernment and insight into our life situations. We will begin to see things from His perspective. This happens when we prayerfully think about what the Bible is saying and how it applies to us.

I am not speaking of an exercise that we get through so we can say we have done it. We read God's Word with an open heart because we want to know His truth. When we do this, God responds. This is a time of fellowship with Him. The importance we place on wanting to hear from God often determines how much we receive from our time with Him. Proverbs tells us how to seek God's wisdom:

My son, if you receive my words, and treasure my commands within you, so that you incline your ear to wisdom, and apply your heart to understanding; yes, if you cry out for discernment, and lift up your voice for understanding, if you seek her as silver, and search for her as for hidden treasures; then you will understand the fear of the LORD, and find the knowledge of God. For the LORD gives wisdom; from His mouth come knowledge and understanding; He stores up sound wisdom for the upright; He is a shield to those who walk uprightly. (Proverbs 2:1-7)

This is a really great scripture. It says He stores up sound wisdom for you and me. In His storehouse, He has set aside wisdom for you and you need to pursue Him to get it. It is yours for the asking and taking. His truth makes us free as we grasp it and claim it for our lives. *"If you abide in My word, you are My disciples indeed. And you shall know the truth, and the truth shall make you free"* (John 8:32-32).

Knowing and understanding the truth about what God has for us, and then claiming it personally, causes God's Spirit to be released to accomplish it. As we agree with God, His Spirit will move on our behalf. Often, when we decide to start praying over an area to become free, a time of prayer and fasting can bring greater illumination, and we may be able to hear God's voice more clearly. Consider setting aside a day to pray and fast and seek God. If you have to work, you may be able to fast breakfast and lunch and during those meal times spend that time calling on God to bring you insight, understanding, and deliverance. Open your heart to Him and be open to hear what He might impress upon you.

Deliverance Is Ours

God has provided deliverance through the work Jesus did for us, and He wants us to walk in that freedom. The hope is not in us, but in Him. It is not our strength, but His.

Always remember that He loves you and He redeemed you from sin and its power. He wants good for you. Joy, peace, and

His love are part of your inheritance. He works in you to set you free from anything that hinders you in your relationship with Him and from obtaining all He has for you.

QUESTIONS FOR REFLECTION AND DISCUSSION

1. Can you identify any areas where healing is needed in your life? List them below.

   _____
   _____
   _____
   _____

2. Are you willing to completely open your heart to God for Him to reveal any truth He desires to reveal to you? What do you sense Him saying to you now?

   _____
   _____
   _____
   _____

3. Are you willing to surrender to Him and ask His Spirit to begin to work in your life? What might that look like?

   _____
   _____
   _____
   _____

(To take a real step toward freedom, take the time to work through the "Worksheet for Freedom" below.)

TAKE A KNEE

Let's pray: *"Dear Father, please do Your work in me. Set me free by Your truth and the power of Your Spirit. I choose to trust You and surrender to You to work as You see fit. I confess that You want only good for my life. I confess that You love me and desire deeper fellowship with me."*

Worksheet for Freedom

Take a Stand for Freedom

1. What stronghold(s) do you sense God wants you to be aware of? Spend time in prayer and ask Him to impress upon you any areas He wants to work in your life and bring greater freedom. Write them down as His Spirit impresses them on your mind.

   _____
   _____
   _____
   _____

2. Ask God, "Show me why this stronghold is in my life. Show me if I am allowing it to be there by my actions or attitudes. How has this affected my life? Give me any insight I need to understand the steps I must take to be free of this."

   Note what He brings to your heart and mind in response and write them down. You might want to pray about this for a number of days until you believe you have received the insight God wants you to have. God honors our persistence in seeking Him about important matters. He delights in us calling out to Him for help in our time of need.

   _____
   _____
   _____
   _____

3. Confess God's love for you, His forgiveness, and His grace given to you. Ask God for His healing. Begin to thank Him

for the victory He is granting. Speak the truth of God's Word aloud. Declare it is for you.

Your prayer might sound like this:

Father, I want to be free from any strongholds I am struggling with. I give this stronghold to You _____ [state it]. I ask You to deliver me.

I confess that I have sinned in this area by _____ [name any thoughts or attitudes you have harbored in your heart or mind against God or others, or actions you have taken].

I purpose right now to begin to seek You for healing and total deliverance from these areas of sin and for healing from any hurts. I know You love me and want me to be free. I also confess and agree with Your Word that You have provided deliverance for me by the work of Jesus on the cross.

I plead the name and blood of Jesus over me and state that I will no longer defile myself by my attitudes or actions. I WILL pray daily, several times a day if needed, over this area of my life. I claim my freedom and healing and will not let Satan deprive me of it with his lies and seduction. Father, I need You more than anything. Thank You for Your love and deliverance.

Stand in Your Freedom

- At what part of the day will you now begin to pray over this area? Write your plan below.

_____

_____

- What truths of Scripture deal with this life issue? List passages below. If you don't know references, ask someone to help you find relevant passages.

- What actions or steps will you need to take to begin to stand in freedom?

Chapter 3

Learning to Stand in Freedom

We not only need to get free from strongholds, we need to stay free. As God reveals and breaks down strongholds in our lives and we begin to experience freedom, then we need to continue to stand in that freedom and experience greater fellowship with God and His love.

Jesus said, *"Take my yoke upon you, and learn from me, for I am gentle and lowly in heart, and you will find rest for your souls. For my yoke is easy and my burden is light"* (Matthew 11:29-30). When we learn from Him, we will find His yoke of walking with Him "light" and "easy." While some may paint a picture of God as being harsh and impossible to please, the Bible says He is gentle and lowly in heart. Wanting to give us rest for our souls. Yes, He wants to heal us and give us peace and inner rest.

One night I was going home on the freeway after a long day at work. On this night, my thinking turned to how God worked in my life and how at times I had to learn things the hard way. It dawned on me that either I could learn by God having to do whatever was necessary to get my attention, or I could open my heart and do all I could to facilitate the process by pursuing God for His truth and the changes He wanted to bring in my life. I wanted to pursue being transformed into the image (character) of Christ. Because God loves me, He will pursue me. But I also need to pursue Him with an open heart.

I decided to go after God more aggressively and open my heart in a greater way, rather than continue to learn by the "two by four" method. That's when someone has to whack us over the head with a two-inch by four-inch stick of wood in order to get our attention. OUCH! That is painful. It's better, and much easier on us, to trust God with our lives and seek Him with open hearts. (I have had numerous lumps and bruises from the two by four method that life can bring. It's not fun. I think I have a few lumps that still linger!)

I prayed, "Father, change my heart and renew my mind. Make me like Christ. Where I have defeated thinking, change me. Help me to be all you want me to be." I began to pray that prayer regularly. As I pursued God and wanted what He desired for me, He responded by speaking to me, revealing things to me, and changing me. When we come to God in this way with an open heart, we guard against strongholds forming again in us.

Satan wants to plant seeds of distrust of God in our heart. He wants us to fear God and to be reluctant to trust Him. But God wants only good for us.

Stand Firm

Scripture has much to say about protecting ourselves against temptation and standing firm against the attack of the enemy. For example, Ephesians 6 is devoted to standing in Christ.

> *Finally, my brethren, be strong in the Lord and in the power of His might. Put on the whole armor of God that you may be able to stand against the wiles of the devil. For we do not wrestle against flesh and blood, but against principalities, against powers, against the rulers of the darkness of this age, against spiritual hosts of wickedness in the heavenly places. Therefore take up the whole armor of God that you may be able to withstand in the evil day, and **having done all, to stand**. (Ephesians 6:10-13, emphasis added)*

The reason it is so important to continue to stand is because thoughts and temptations—sudden urges to do wrong or fall back into old sin patterns—continue to come from the world around us and from the enemy. However, we are not left unprotected against these attacks. The following verses tell us about strategic pieces of armor that will protect us.

> *Stand therefore, having girded your waist with truth, having put on the breastplate of righteousness, and having shod your feet with the preparation of the gospel of peace; above all, taking the shield of faith with which you will be able to quench all the fiery darts of the wicked one. And take the helmet of salvation, and the sword of the Spirit, which is the word of God; praying always with all prayer and supplication in the Spirit, being watchful to this end with all perseverance and supplication for all the saints.* (Ephesians 6:14-18)

Let's look at two of these pieces of armor that are of special value as we stand firm against the formation or restoration of strongholds.

The Helmet of Salvation

Putting on the "helmet of salvation" means that we do not allow our minds to think ungodly, immoral, or unhealthy thoughts. A helmet is to protect our head. So we have to protect our minds against unhealthy thinking. This not only protects us, it changes us. What we allow ourselves to think about is crucial to our well-being.

What we take in with our eyes, ears and thoughts, affect our life. We need to think according to our new lives in Christ—our salvation lives—not our old ones. Philippians 4:8 tells us what to think about:

> *Finally, brothers, whatever is true, whatever is honorable, whatever is just, whatever is pure, whatever is lovely, whatever is commendable, if there is any excellence, if there is anything worthy of praise, think about these things. (Philippians 4:8)*

Our lives can often be changed simply by changing our thinking. This does not mean unhealthy or ungodly thoughts will never enter our minds. The enemy is capable of putting those thoughts there. But once we realize what we are thinking about, we can make the choice to stop thinking those thoughts and instead think on what is true, honorable, just, pure, lovely, and commendable. In other words, put out the bad and think on the good. You can do this. All of us can.

We can control what we think about. We can choose not to think about one thing and instead choose to think about something else. If this were not true, God would not tell us to do so. There are times when we come under demonic attack in our minds. The thoughts may seem strong and persistent, but we are given weapons to dispel those thoughts and the enemy. When this happens, you can plead the blood of Jesus over your thoughts and command the enemy to leave you. You can quote Scripture over you and defeat the enemy. The Bible states, *"Submit therefore to God. Resist the devil and he will flee from you"* (James 4:7). We have the authority from God to not only resist the devil, but to order him to flee from us. We can take this stand and watch the demonic attack leave us. It may happen immediately or take a few minutes of taking this stand. But he will have to leave.

Practicing "right thinking" will transform you. It will change not only your thinking, but your attitudes and actions! Agreeing with God in our thinking brings the activity of the Holy Spirit into our lives in a greater way. It stirs up the activity of His Spirit in us. Remember, the Bible states, *"Do not be conformed to this world, but be transformed by the renewing of your mind, that you may prove what is that good and acceptable will of God"* (Romans 12:2). Thinking right brings opportunities to act right. Acting right will cause the Holy Spirit to flow through us in a greater manner. The more we choose to not allow wrong or sinful thinking to remain in our minds, the more we will live differently. We will have more joy and love in our lives.

The Holy Spirit's flow will increase our influence and allow us to affect others positively. We can become a life-giving person. Imagine all you can do if you go around thinking right all of the time—or even most of the time. Think of how it will change you and the effect it will have on those around you.

The transformation happening *in* us will flow *out* of us. The Holy Spirit will begin to move in a greater way in our lives because He now has a more open channel to flow through, one that is not blocked by hindering thoughts and attitudes. You will like this difference; it is infectious!

Another aspect of the "helmet of salvation" has to do with the following passage in Hebrews 10:

> *Therefore, brethren, having boldness to enter the Holiest by the blood of Jesus, by a new and living way which He consecrated for us, through the veil, that is His flesh, and having a High Priest over the house of God, let us draw near with a*

true heart in full assurance of faith, having our hearts sprinkled from an evil conscience and our bodies washed with pure water. (Verses 19-22)

These verses speak of an "evil conscience." The word *conscience* in the New Testament comes from a Greek word that means "to comprehend or realize." Our conscience helps us comprehend and realize what we are doing in light of what is right. A conscience is a good thing. God's Spirit works in conjunction with our conscience to lead us, guide us, and keep us from evil or harmful things.

So, what is an evil conscience? An evil conscience is one that condemns us, brings up our faults, shortcomings, and past deeds, and tells us we have little or no value. An evil conscience is one that holds us down, discourages us, and makes us feel like we are slime. It says we are unworthy and should not expect anything good from God.

However, the Hebrews passage says we are to *"draw near with a true heart in full assurance of faith, having our hearts sprinkled from an evil conscience"* (verse 22). We must have the assurance that we are clean and are in right standing with God due to the work of Jesus.

We have been sprinkled with His blood, forgiven of all. We stand clean before our God and heavenly Father and have fellowship with Him. If God's Spirit convicts us of wrongdoing or sin, we confess it and ask forgiveness—and we are forgiven. We are freed from an "evil conscience" and can draw near "with assurance," even in boldness, knowing that Jesus has made us right with God.

We must stand against an "evil conscience." God does not accuse us, the enemy does. God wants to build us up and not tear us down. God says, *"For I know the thoughts I think toward you . . . thoughts of peace and not of evil, to give you a future and a hope"*

(Jeremiah 29:11, NKJV). He has a "future and hope" for us. We must not give in to an evil conscience, but walk in His assurance knowing God loves us and has purpose for us.

The Breastplate of Righteousness

Another piece of armor that God has given us is the "breastplate of righteousness." This means to guard our hearts with righteousness. The breastplate went over the chest to protect the vital organs, and the heart is the most vital organ. "*Guard your heart,*" Proverbs 4:23 says, *"Keep [guard] your heart with all vigilance, for from it flow the springs of life."*

What is in our hearts flows out into our entire beings and becomes a part of us. We cannot help this, it will happen. That's why the Scriptures urge us to be vigilant to guard or watch over our heart, our desire center. We want to keep it free of things that will bring harm to our lives, things like hurt, bitterness, lust, a critical spirit, fear, and anything else that is unscriptural, immoral, and unhealthy.

We need to see our hearts as soil in which we will allow only good seeds to be planted. When we realize that any of these things are trying to take root in our hearts, we confess them and ask God to remove them. Then, we stand against the thoughts or attitudes that are trying to plant bad seeds in our hearts. This is how we guard our hearts.

Guard with righteousness. There are two components to righteousness. First, the Bible says we are made righteous by accepting Christ in our lives. His righteousness then is "imputed" to us, or becomes a part of us. When God sees us, He sees the same righteousness Jesus has.

But the Bible also talks about walking in righteousness. This means we go through our lives confident of our standing in

Christ. When the enemy tries to accuse us, we can state that we have been made righteous in Christ. Even though we fail at times, Jesus' work in us settles the issue of who we are and our standing in Him.

Part of walking in righteousness is our behavior. The Apostle Paul prayed that the believers in the church in Colossae would *"have a walk worthy of the Lord, fully pleasing Him, being fruitful in every good work and increasing in the knowledge of God"* (Colossians 1:9-10).

A person desiring to live a righteous life is one who chooses to seek God, obey Him, and live by God's standards. Righteous or "right" acts include believing the truth, obeying God's Word and His revealed will, and acting toward others as God would have us to. We develop these good habits by practicing them.

As we practice them. we will be strengthened in all areas of our lives. Past areas of bondage can actually become areas of strength as we persist in praying and learning to stand in the freedom Christ has provided. God, through Jesus, has provided us with a transformed life. But now we are to practice the transformed life. We are to choose to live in what Jesus has provided for us.

The Decision to Stand for God

Though God has provided the armor we need in order to guard our hearts and stand in our freedom, we face a choice whether to put it on and walk in God's ways, or go along with the ways of thinking and acting we see around us.

The world tells us many things in life are acceptable that the Bible tells us are not. If we compromise and live according to the world's standards instead of God's standards, it will affect and afflict our lives.

If we traffic in worldly things, we will lose our spiritual appetites and will open ourselves up to compromise. Our hearts will lose their passion for God and His ways. Trafficking in the world's ways opens us up to a hardened heart, and to strongholds redeveloping in our lives.

Leviticus 10:10 tells us we are to *"distinguish between the holy and unholy, between the clean and unclean, and that you may teach the children of Israel all the statutes which the Lord has spoken to them by the hand of Moses".* We do this by knowing what God's Word says and obeying it. Romans 12:1-2 says,

> *"I beseech you therefore brethren, by the mercies of God, that you present your bodies a living sacrifice, holy, acceptable to God, which is your reasonable service. And do not be conformed to this world, but be transformed by the renewing of your mind, that you may prove what is that good and acceptable will of God."*

We are not to be taken in by the world or live our lives according to the world's standards.

> *Do not love the world or the things in the world. If anyone loves the world, the love of the Father is not in him. For all that is in the world-the lust of the flesh, the lust of the eyes, and the pride of life-is not of the Father but is of the world. (1 John 2:15-16)*

We are to live by God's truth, not the world's "truth." We are told to "flee" from the thinking and things of the world (1 Timothy 6:11). We are in this world, but we are not to live according to its thinking when it conflicts with God's teachings. God's ways bring peace in our souls, even in the midst of a world that can be cruel and corrupt, as these verses show.

> *As you have therefore received Christ Jesus the Lord, so walk in Him, rooted and built up in Him and established in the faith, as you have been taught, abounding in it with thanksgiving. Beware lest anyone cheat you through philosophy and empty deceit, according to the tradition of men, according to the basic principles of the world, and not according to Christ.*
>
> *In Him you were also circumcised with the circumcision made without hands, by putting off the body of the sins of the flesh, by the circumcision of Christ, buried with Him in baptism, in which you also were raised with Him through faith in the working of God, who raised Him from the dead.*
>
> *And you, being dead in your trespasses and the uncircumcision of your flesh, He has made alive together with Him, having forgiven you all trespasses, having wiped out the handwriting of requirements that was against us, which was contrary to us. And He has taken it out of the way, having nailed it to the cross. Having disarmed principalities and powers, He made a public spectacle of them, triumphing over them. (Colossians 2:6-15)*

God has disarmed the enemy and has made provision for you to walk and live in that victory. His freedom is for you! We fight from a position of victory—His victory!

God's Provision for Ongoing Victory

Romans 7 talks about our flesh, the part of us that is drawn to sin, battling against our new self. Romans 8 says that we can win this battle because of God's Spirit in us to empower us to stand against the flesh. Ephesians 6 speaks about our enemy trying to seduce us and defeat us.

So, whether we are battling the flesh or the enemy, God has provided what we need to win through the work of Christ on the cross. Will we stumble at times? Yes. But that is not a reason to excuse ourselves or develop a way of life that accepts our old nature as a normal way of life for a Christian.

We may stumble, but we get back up, pray over our failures, and ask God to continue to change us and strengthen us. This process is part of life. The good news is, God is always there. He loves us, and as we go through life we can be joyful knowing He will never leave us or forsake us (Hebrews 13:5). Though we may battle at times, He has provided all we need.

QUESTIONS FOR REFLECTION AND DISCUSSION

1. What stronghold, if any, has God been bringing to your mind during this study?

   _____

2. What types of thoughts or temptations do you battle? What is your resolve to overcome them?

   _____

3. What have you learned from this chapter about what you can do at those times?

_____
_____
_____
_____

4. How do you need to guard your heart in this area?

_____
_____
_____

(If you haven't already, use the Freedom Worksheet at the end of the previous chapter regarding this area.)

TAKE A KNEE

Let's pray: "*God, help me to stand today. May Your Spirit move on me and prompt me about the way I should walk today, all day long. May my attitudes be right, and my mind fixed on You and Your will for me. Whenever my mind begins to stray, bring me back. Whenever my heart begins to stray, bring me back. I pray for the Holy Spirit to lead me though this day and to draw me to You all during the day.*"

Chapter 4

THE STRONGHOLD OF PORNOGRAPHY

God has given us everything we need to bring down all strongholds, including one of the most prevalent and destructive in the world today. As we look at our weapons for the war against strongholds, let's look at the battle for freedom from the specific stronghold of pornography, one of the greatest seducers of both men and women today. Because it is so prevalent today, I want to take time to address this area.

Pornography is easily available. In fact, it is thrown at us. It makes sexual sin look exciting and appealing. It feeds the flesh, stirring up lust and causing us to compromise standards God gave us to protect us, our families, and our culture.

Pornography has become a powerful, destructive stronghold for millions of people, wreaking havoc in their lives. It is affecting Christians' and churches' thinking, and causing us to accept immorality as normal. It is destroying marriages, destroying pastors and churches, and giving rise to sexual and lifestyle perversion in untold numbers of lives.

The lie of pornography is that it will satisfy us. The opposite is true. There is no satisfaction in pornography. It stirs up lust, causes your love for your mate to diminish, hurts your marriage, and affects your children. If you are single, it can causes you to live in lust and can lead you to pursue immoral relationships (please read Proverbs chapter 5).

It also causes your love for God to wane and can deeply affect your relationship with Him. Participating in pornography can cause you to become a vessel burning with lust and your mind to be filled with thoughts of immorality and desires to participate in sexual acts with women you do not even know and will never know; they are just images doing sexual acts. You cannot have a zeal for God when you are burning with lust.

Husbands and fathers must realize that even if they practice this in secret, the door opens for Satan to attack their children and wives. As men, we are supposed to be the spiritual leaders in our homes. That is God's standard. If we as leaders practice an area of immorality, it will affect our families. Our "spiritual covering" over them has been breached.

I have met couples who have divorced because of pornography. Families have been torn apart by it, and fathers have passed along this sin to sons. I have known of wives who have confessed that their sexual relationship with their husbands has become almost nonexistent, only to discover that their husbands were involved in pornography. Pornography will distort your thinking, your actions, and your love of your wife and children—and you may end up spiritually shipwrecked.

One cannot traffic in pornography and walk with God in holiness and fellowship. Those who have been captivated by pornography must be freed—and they can be freed. The battle against the stronghold of pornography begins at the same starting point as that of other strongholds:

1. Want Freedom

Like our story about Ted who was trapped in immoral relationships, we will only get free if we truly want to. If we enjoy pornography and continue to view it, it simply means we are not ready to give it up. Viewing pornography is a decision a person makes. No one is forcing you to do so. It is your decision. *Until we want to be free, we won't be free.*

An older Christian man I knew was meeting with a younger man to counsel him. The younger man began to say he was involved in pornography and couldn't get free. He said he felt trapped and bound.

The older man looked at him, and told him, "If you truly want to be free, you can be free. You obviously do not realize the work Christ did for you on the cross. He gave you the ability to be free from sin. It's possible you are believing a lie the enemy has told you that you can't be free; that this sin is too strong for you to overcome. Or, it's possible that you like your sin and are not ready to give it up. But to say you can't be free is wrong. It flies in the face of biblical truth. I challenge you to open your heart to God and begin to bathe this area in prayer. Ask God to change your heart and change your thinking. He will. If you want to be free, you can be."

I realize millions are struggling in this area. However, either God's Word is true or not. Either you have been redeemed from sin or you have not. If you are indulging in this sin, you are choosing to and you are not appropriating God's provision for freedom in this area.

This sin, this stronghold, can be broken and you can live in freedom. God has provided for your victory, but you must pursue Him for it. The day we became saved, became a Christian, we obtained all we needed to live a victorious life. But we must learn what is ours and appropriate it. We need to search Scripture and realize Christ set us free! We must go after the victory that is ours by prayer and trusting God for the victory.

If pornography is a stronghold in your life, decide right now, this moment, to begin to get freedom. Get serious!

2. Engage the Battle

Tell God you want to be free and determine to **continue to seek God and stand with Him until the bondage is broken.** This stronghold will require more than just a simple prayer. As we have discussed, in any area of bondage, including pornography, you should cry out to God to change you by changing your heart and desires and renewing your mind. When you ask Him to break this bondage, He will, and then you must learn to stand in your freedom.

This needs to be a **daily matter of prayer.** Call upon Him each time you are tempted. When the enemy comes in like a flood, you may feel overwhelmed by temptation and lust. But if you cry out to God with an open heart when this happens, the enemy will be defeated and will flee from you. James 4:7 says, *"Therefore submit to God. Resist the devil and he will flee from you. Draw near to God and He will draw near to you. Cleanse your hands, you sinners; and purify your hearts, you double-minded."*

If you have to pray about it off and on during the day, so be it. As you do this, the battle will lesson, though temptations will still come.

Begin to **focus on God's truth.** God's purpose is for your normal sexual desires to be fulfilled with one woman—your wife.

Drink water from your own cistern, and running water from your own well. Should your fountains be dispersed abroad, streams of water in the streets? Let them be only your own, and not for strangers with you. Let your fountain be blessed and rejoice with the wife of your youth. As a loving deer and graceful doe, let her breasts satisfy you at all times; and always be enraptured with her love. For why should you, my son, be enraptured by an immoral woman, and be embraced in the arms of a seductress? (Proverbs 5:15-20)

I watched a TV interview with an actress involved in pornography. They spoke to her about her life and the movies she made. The interviewer asked if her personal sex life was like the movies. "No," she said, "That is acting, and I'm paid to do those things. My real life is different."

When men watch pornography, they are watching fantasy, yet they then expect their wives to live up to that fantasy. It's unrealistic. They are getting expectations that are not real and putting those expectations on their wives. But if you love your wife and ask God to show you how to love her, both physically and through your actions and words, you can have a great love life with her. God wants you to love your wife and He wants you and her to experience a fulfilling love life.

As a man focuses on loving his wife, delighting in her, and desiring her, she can offer something no other woman can—a sexual relationship based upon love that is blessed by God. If you want to be fulfilled sexually, love your wife.*

---

* (For more on this subject, please see the study in this series, *A Man and Sex.*)

Continue to pray that any desire you have for pornography will be taken away. Ask God to cleanse your heart and change it. He will! When we continue to ask God to change our hearts and renew our minds, we will find He is faithful! I urge you: do not be the slave to any bondage, including pornography. You can be free. You don't have to let pornography destroy you and your family. You don't have to be bound in this area. God wants you to be free and walk in freedom, and to use the spiritual weapons He has given you to sustain that freedom.

A FINAL WORD

Freedom from any stronghold will only happen when we want to be free. We cannot enjoy our sin, pursue it, and expect God to deliver us. He can and will deliver us, and even change our hearts' desires regarding it, but we must be honest with ourselves and Him, and pursue Him for this. We must agree with God about our life.

Much of what we gain in our walk with God comes from laying hold of His promises for us after we realize what they are. Until we realize God's will for us and come into agreement about it, we may continue to live out our old life instead of the new life Christ has for us.

We have an active part in living and growing in Him and gaining all He has for us. He does the work as we desire it and seek Him for it. If we want our old life more than our new one, which we have been given in Christ, we will settle for less and continue to live in it. Or, if we like our sin or are complacent about it, we will not conquer it. Jesus has conquered all sin, and He wants us to enter into that victory. We must agree, let Him change our hearts, and free us.

Remember, God wants us to be free and to walk in freedom. His work was not in vain, it was for us. Celebrate His work by walking in His truth.

ABOUT THE AUTHOR

Lou Turner wrote the "Living Life God's Way" series out of his passion for men to discover God, and to get to know Him and what He has for them. This 13-book men's discipleship series is the culmination of Lou's own journey—a life of seeking God, studying His Word, memorizing Scripture and meditating on it, and practical experience with family, community, marketplace work, and Christian ministry. It also comes, by Lou's own admission, from life experiences of both successes and mistakes, as a result of both good and bad decisions.

Lou has headed ministries, written and taught workshops, classes, and seminars, and discipled dozens of men. Now, he has put into print the things he has learned to help other men along their path and journey.

Most of Lou's growing up years were spent in Detroit and its suburbs, where he was raised in a pastor's home. Following his graduation from university with a Bachelor of Science in Business Administration, Lou and his wife planted and pastored a church for three years. After that time, he felt the strong call of God to return to business.

Over the years, Lou has served in numerous senior executive positions with national and international companies in the real estate and oil and gas industries. As of this writing, Lou is still active in business with his own home building company. He has

ABOUT THE AUTHOR

been married to his wife Joan since they were 20. They have three children and 10 grandchildren and make their home in Phoenix, Arizona.

www.ingramcontent.com/pod-product-compliance
Lightning Source LLC
Chambersburg PA
CBHW021123080526
44587CB00010B/613